The Benefits of a Bully Wraith War

L.A. Kendrick

ISBN for Paperback: 979-8-89496-797-4

ISBN for eBook: 979-8-89496-798-1

Table of Contents

INTRODUCTION

I'm running as fast as I can, out of breath, but I've got to keep going. The corn is high; these stalks are slapping my face. I hear the rest of the gang with me; then I hear them scream and silence. We've got to get away, got to keep moving. From what I can listen to, there's only one more of us left, plus me. I turn to look; I can see the corn stalks moving in my direction. That's the last one. Is it Sterling, Dexter, Turkeesha, or Derron? I yell out, "This way," but I'm still booking it to get out and away from the cornfield. Then I hear no more movements. I yell everyone's name, but nothing; no one says anything back.

Then I see the corn stalks fly into the air as if they're being spit out by a giant mower. Something big, or strong, is coming my way. I catch my second wind and sprint, but my Gyro shoes aren't working. I don't have my slingshots. I've got nothing to fight back with; all I have is hope. And then I see an opening at the end of the cornfield on the left. I break for it and turn to the left, but this thing is closing on me. I'm finally out. I look back, and the only thing I can compare this thing to is a ball of fast-moving laundry clothes with everything from hats to old jackets, just a nightmare.

I run towards the bridge that will get me home, and I hear the name repeatedly: Satchel Crowson. And that thing is bearing down on me. It's starting to take shape, like a man flying with a large sack. Oh man, I've just got to make it to the bridge. Darn, my shoes are still not working, but at least I made it to the bridge. The bridge is spinning around; I can't catch my balance. I fall. I can't move; it's like I'm being crushed. Arms of Ogun, don't let this thing get me. It's got my leg lifting and putting me inside the bag. I can see everybody's faces, including my friends, at the bottom of the bag. They look terrified. I'm getting put in, too. I'm falling faster and faster, about to hit the bottom. Can't stop… NOOOOOOOOOOOOOO!

"Son, son, are you alright? What's going on?" my dad says, running in. He's in a fighting stance, looking around the room. My dad's a great fighter. I was having a nightmare, the worst kind, Dad. I'm sweating and still shaking. He comes over and sits on the bed. I lean on him; he is my protector. He puts his hand on my right shoulder and tells me it's ok; let's talk about it in the morning. He leaves, but not before looking around my room and shutting the door. That was strange for him to do. We've got problems, big, creepy problems. Let me steady myself. I'm Sedale… Sedale Johnson. In the morning, I will rally the troops because something wicked this way runs!

Chapter 1

Tara Waddell

Waking up, I slowly open my eyes to the ceiling fan spinning, trying to forget and remember that dream from last night. What did it mean? I was taught at the academy that dreams are not just portals into our souls but into other realms. Sometimes, things try to communicate with us or take us from here, where we live, into wherever dream lane can go. So, I get up, head hurting a bit, but I look out the window and see my dad outside shooting hoops. He's hitting shot after shot without a miss. I run to the bathroom, brush my teeth, and wash up, eager to get a game or two in with my dad. I hurried downstairs and said to my mother, "Morning, Mom," as she made Breakfast.

Now, my dad is killing the rim with dunk after powerful dunk. He's a serious athlete, more than I thought. Now I see why he made that full-court basketball court. This is where the men go and talk, but in this case, father and son.

So, I greet my dad as I was taught: always greet adults. He passes me the ball and says, "Show me what you got, and let's talk about that dream or nightmare you had last night," he says while getting into a defensive stance.

I try to drive to the goal, and he cuts me off. I backed out and tried it again, and the same thing happened. So, I pulled up for a jump shot, and you guessed it, he blocked it hard. Then it was his turn; he posted me up... score. I told him that it was unfair; he had the size advantage. Then he just started pulling up jumper after jumper until it was 21. He yells out, "GAME," while raising an eyebrow.

Now, he goes over the defense and sets how to get better. He then asks me about the dream. I tell him it was cornfields, me and the fellas, this floating thing chasing us; the name Satchel Crowson kept popping up in the nightmare. I don't know that name, though, Dad.

My dad looks puzzled and says, "Dreams, be they nightmares, always have a meaning. It's the mind's way of releasing tension. Without dreams, we would go crazy," he says. As he passed me the ball, I started to think, but then Derron, my friend and neighbor, joined us. We've been running around since we were in diapers.

So, he's here. Then he greets my dad with, "Mr. Johnson, sir." His parents are the same as mine; they don't play the disrespect thing. My dad has told me that having respect and showing it could save my life in many tough spots. We try to double-team him in 21, even though it's an everyman-for-himself style of basketball. He destroys us; it isn't even close.

Derron tells my dad, "You could let us win at least one game." But my dad responds dad's, "Now, what's the fun in that? These life lessons will shape you, improve you, teach you to take on challenges, help you earn victories, and build your character. We are losing our youth by rewarding, not trying. Inventions are made with effort, translating into trying if you, young cats, get my point."

We do, and I say, "One day, I will beat you. I'm going to practice as often as I can. Then, before you know it, I will be the one yelling 'game,' Dad."

He smiles. "Now that's what I'm talking about. Never lay down for anybody. Always stay educated and fit, and keep boundaries that you will not compromise," he says as he prepares for the guys who have been trying to beat him for months. And here they are: one is a Division 1 college basketball player, the other, I think he said, just recently retired from the NBA like last season. Both are at least 6 ft tall and in great shape.

"This is gonna be good," Derron says as we sit down, trying to find tips for beating my dad. They shoot for it; the first to hit has the first ball. They all swish the net. This goes on for a few minutes as they trash-talk each other. The ex-pro is the first to miss. Now it's just my dad and the D-1. D-1 misses, and my dad swishes. Now they go at it; my dad pulls up jumper after jumper, nothing but net. So now they try to double and trap Dad, but he has handles and splits the D for a monster dunk. He gets the ball back, then quickly takes the ex-pro into the low post. It reminds me of James Worthy from old footage. Dad holds the ball high in his right hand, looking over his shoulders, left then right, to ensure he beats the trap. He spins left so quickly that the ex-pro falls, and D-1 is dunked on. "OOOOOOOOOOOOOOH," we yell.

This goes on for about an hour. My dad's blocking shot after shot, stealing the ball, rebounding, and has hardly broken a sweat. The closest thing that I've seen that even comes close to what my dad is doing was Mr. Brown when he saved my butt a few missions back… wait, who am I trying to fool? I've never seen anything like what Mr. Brown did to that thing that tried to kill me. That was straight special.

Dad yells, "Game!" They all forearm bump and say, "Next time." Then Mom comes out and says, "Breakfast is ready. Go wash your hands with soap and water, and let's eat." "Yes, ma'am," we reply. Once we do, we come out to the table. Mom has a great spread: turkey bacon, sausage, egg whites, fruits, cranberry juice, orange juice, and biscuits. We bow our heads and give thanks; then we dig in. It's always a great time because Mom is the best cook ever.

Now, my parents are hugging again, and my dad kisses my mom on her cheek. I've never seen them argue. Maybe they do it when I'm not around. They always seem to be putting others' needs before their own. Anyway, a special news bulletin just came on the TV. It looks serious because my parents snap to attention when it comes across the screen with the report. Oh, this should be good—another mission for The Battle Boyz. Aww, yeah, let's see where the getdown goes. A lady and a man get their papers ready to read. Here goes.

Chapter 2

Gene Childs

Hello, and good morning, everyone. I'm reporter Tara Waddell, bringing you this BREAKING NEWS STORY. A strange condition has befallen the town; it has caused hallucinations, sleepwalking, sleep paralysis, nightmares, night terrors, and a rash that covers large portions of the body. We have information about what has been called ground zero. Our local reporter, Marvin Hardy, is on the scene. Marvin…

"Well, thank you, Tara. It has been a most unusual case, to say the least, one of the most unusual in all my years of reporting. Now, what you see behind me is where it all started. Yep, our local movie theater is the biggest one in the city, to be correct. The hospitals say that most of the patients they have received have been admitted a day or two after coming from the movies. Why, you might ask? What is the culprit? Well, none other than, you guessed it, 'Popcorn.' Yes, viewers, you heard me right. Now, the CDC has stepped in and closed down the movie theater, while the scientists have uncovered spores that contain GMOs (Genetically Modified Organisms) down to the DNA. Now, because the blockbuster film 'The Trials Of Shabazz' has been keeping the building packed to capacity for two months, the popcorn deliveries couldn't keep up, so they ran out. Until a local farmer named Satchel Crowson offered his local brand and saved the day, but that's when people started to experience all of the symptoms.

The local manager, Gene Childs, stated that he had called around town, and a few other businesses had done business with Mr. Crowson, and he checked out fine, so he saw no reason to doubt his corn. Even though he's lived here all his life, he had never heard of Mr. Crowson.

Here's what he had to say:

'I was looking for a way to keep up with the popcorn demand, so I went local. This mistake was terrible; I've already been hit with several lawsuits. I hope they find the guy; this is a bad day for the town,' Manager Gene says.

Now, the authorities have been looking for Mr. Crowson, but upon arriving at his farm, they found his house was on fire and had burnt to the ground, with Mr. Crowson nowhere to be seen.

Also, please take a close look behind me; a few acres of corn should have burned as well, as they are in such proximity to the house, but strangely, they are untouched. For now, the story keeps piling up more questions than answers. I turn it back over to you, Tara."

This is turning out to be a bizarre case, but stay tuned to See Me TV, and we will keep you posted on the latest developments in this story. But in the meantime, if you have eaten popcorn from this place, see your family doctor or ER because the symptoms from the studies affect people differently. This has been Tara Waddell for "See Me TV," channel three news.

So that explains it; we all ate the popcorn last night. Mom ate a lot, and so did Derron. I'm the fellas, and I'm still determining, but I've texted them, and they're saying they ate other stuff but no popcorn. I noticed my dad had this concerned look for my mom. She moves her shirt over so that he can see her shoulder, and yep, there is a rash. She had bad dreams too last night, so Dad goes to the bathroom and returns with a remedy that's been in his family for, like, forever. He rubs it on her shoulder, and she makes a face at first, then relaxes and smiles.

Then, Dad gives her a drink. He starts explaining what's in it because Mom is asking. I take a napkin and start writing down what he says; well, I do my best, some words I've never heard: Echinacea, aloe vera water, elderberry, vitamin C, vitamin E, honey, and cranberry juice. He says, "We'll clear you up from the inside out. I promise this will clear you up in a few days or sooner!" Dad says.

So, she drinks up and likes the flavor. So they hug each other with a quick laugh; Mom replies, "I feel it working already." Dad raises an eyebrow, asking Mom, "You got jokes, huh?" They start clearing the table. I ask if they need help; they both tell me not this time. I would like to know if I can meet the guys at Rudolph Pettus Park. Dad says yes, but let us know when you get there; hit us with a text or voice message.

"Hold up, wait a minute. Take Roscoe some food before you go, and when was the last time you took him for a walk?" my dad asks.

"Yesterday, Pop, remember? Way before we went to the movies. Me and Derron walked him for over 45 minutes at the park. Yes, sir, all over it," I reply.

"Well, make sure you bathe him sometime this week. I will be leaving for work, which is another long trip, so I won't be home when you return. Make sure you're back before sundown. You got the house, young man. Do you have any money on you?" he asks.

"Yes, sir, I do. Thanks," I reply. (We have a card from the Latimer Academy with quite a bit of money, so if we are out and don't have any, we always have some). I won't let him know, but my mother will tell him.

So, me and Derron go outside to feed Roscoe. You guys remember my big Great Dane that saved me and my mom a while back from that thing…In the fog that night, the car caught a flat tire. As we go out, I try to send a message to the Lewis Latimer Academy. Mr. Brown says to let them know if anything weird happens so they can investigate, but I can't get anything out to them. It's just static, no signal. That place has the best tech on the planet. I wondered if the fellas had the same issues, so I sent them texts to see if they had the same problems.

We finished feeding Roscoe and took off for the park. I still determine what game we'll play, but I will win big. The only time I've come close to losing is to that Cootie girl, but Dexter and

Sterling is getting better.

Chapter 3

Alfredia Jackson

With Derron on a skateboard and me on foot, we take off towards the park to build that camaraderie you can only develop with people your age. Don't get me wrong; adults set the rules, but we apply them to all aspects of our young lives. You know what? So far, so good!

When you get out and play, you see the world in ways you never could by sitting in the house or front of a TV, playing video games all day. I'm not saying I don't play video games—don't be ridiculous—but I'm a fella, and I spend way more active time outside. What's even more eye- opening is that when you're reading stories about monsters, ghosts, and aliens, at the time, you think it's a story, something to keep kids in line. But we know the truth: that stuff is real. Now, Derron doesn't know the truth; he's just skating away on his board, hopping here and there, without monster care in the world—at least, not until one of those stories is told. Yes, sir, when you get out and walk with friends in all kinds of weather, you learn to appreciate the small things while building lifelong friendships.

For example, we stop a few feet from the Alfredia Jackson Bridge. There's an anthill; they look swamped. I pull out my magnifying glass—not to burn them, I know what a person might think—but to study them. I angle the glass so it doesn't make a sunbeam. Now, we get to look at the antennae on their heads. You can even see the little hairs on their heads, the pinchers, and the black eyes. Those little boogers are working hard, lifting crumbs from that empty bag of potato chips. Some of them are bigger than the others; they are pretty strong. I read somewhere that they can lift 20 times their weight. That's about 4,000 pounds if you were a human. Can you imagine? I bet they have some way we can at the academy. I saw Mr. Brown tear the arms of that thing that almost had me; he did it quickly. Here I go, thinking again. So, before I drift off too far, we make it to the bridge, sit on the side, and wait for the crew as we watch the river flow under us. I lean back and stare up at the sky, watching the clouds roll by. Derron starts calling out the shapes he thinks the clouds make. Heck, man, we both do while laughing and tossing pebbles in the water. The railing on the bridge makes it almost impossible to fall in accidentally, so we're pretty safe.

So we're enjoying the day when Derron suddenly asks me about NASA missions, just like we used to talk about. He mentioned the Mercury missions and talked about all the crazy things they saw and how long they had to keep secrets, some until their deathbeds, the only time they spoke about what they saw. He asked me why I didn't talk of aliens as much as I used to. Now, I can't tell him the reason is that all of it is true. I can't tell him about the academy, but I tell him I talk about that often. "Check your text messages, but you never respond. Go ahead, check your phone, bro." I forgot I sent them; he's my best friend, and we still hang out often.

"Oh yeah," he says. "Boy, you did send a lot of messages. How did I miss all of these?" He goes on while looking up at the sky with his hand over his eyebrow, trying to block the sunlight from blinding him. "Well, a man had ties with the last Mercury mission astronaut, Gordon Cooper. He says he found a UFO on the ocean floor in the Bermuda Triangle. He has a shipwreck-finding business, guided by maps that Cooper left. I think he said they were just crashed ship coordinates, but he found a spot with an alien crashed spaceship." We both get quiet and start smiling, even though his smile seems weird. I shake it off when we are met with tossed, flopping fish. "Y'all know what this means—the gang's all here."

"Let's get the show on the road, Flop O's," Dexter yells, smiling and being his usual self. He hops on one leg with his hand over his face and makes the letter L with his pointed finger and thumb.

"Hey, 'Mongoose mouth,' you almost hit me with that smelly fish. I sure hope you picked a game today that I can use to check that smile on your face," Derron replies, but not smiling, which again is weird for him; he looks pretty mad.

"Yep, you'll get to 'Dent the Donkey Boy' with the game lined up. Even in vocational school, my older brother still plays with his friends," Sterling says as we walk to the bridge.

"Did you guys get my message about the hero hotline being unable to check out the latest stats?" I ask. That's code for the academy.

They both respond, "Yeah." Dexter gives me a nod and walks close to Derron, giving him a little friendly nudge and keeping him entertained as Sterling and I talk.

"It's extraordinary. They have the best tech on the planet, period. Something's blocking our signals, and it's gotta be powerful to do that," Sterling says as we continue walking under the bridge, looking up at the hidden work we've done to safeguard the area. We have a lot of isolated spots that we prepare just in case we have to be on our own if the academy can't get to us right away.

"We have to keep trying, though. That popcorn rash thing is weird. Did you figure out who Satchel Crowson is? That guy's name popped up in my dream, and the thing in my dream took us all down!" I reply as I kick a rock across the bridge.

"I'm waiting for my database to download the name, so it should be ready by the time we stop playing," Sterling says as we get to the end of the bridge opening. "Aw, man, not this. Poffy Puffs is here. Hey, boys, ready to get trashed?" Turkeesha says, " Oh, look, she's brought another annoying girl. Both of them have this deviant look on their faces. Here we go!

Chapter 4

Marvin Hardy

"Oh God, who asked you to show up here?" I ask as they approach, pounding their fists into their hands.

"Why, Sterling, of course. He wants to make sure that you 'Frog Bumps' have good competition today," Turkeesha says, looking at Sterling and giving him a wink.

All the guys look at Sterling frowningly. I'm pretty sure we're all thinking the same thing: Why did you invite the "Cootie Brigade?"

"What? Hey, fellas, I just thought it might be fun to...you know, mix it up. She is one of the best at the Acad...I mean, at the school?" Sterling replies, almost giving away our secret. I think that he likes her. Yuck!

"Well, somebody's about to get their feelings hurt today. You are not going to take it easy because you're a girl. I won't let any girls get the best of us, right, fellas?" Dexter says, to a group nod of agreement.

We keep going past the cornfield on the right, and a little down is an old steel factory that we also set up as a backup base to fight the baddies, just in case. Staying prepared is vital. As we continued, we saw. Parker, an elder of the community. She always has a stick and bag with her, collecting cans. Quite strange, though, she has a lovely home.

"How are you young people doing today?" Ms. Parker asks, stopping for a few minutes to speak with us.

"We're great, ma'am. How about you?" I reply, glad to see her.

"Good, I'm just out getting my exercise. My husband and I used to walk every day. It's not the same without him, but I must keep going until we meet again. You kids remember: stay fit all your lives, and not just for sports, okay?" she says as she continues past us.

"I love that lady. She's a widow now that she lost her husband a few months back. Mom says it would be like losing your best friend. Must be hard on her," Turkeesha says as we continue to the park.

"Whenever I see her, I think she's like some cool secret agent. You guys know what I mean? A low-key secret agent," Dexter says, adjusting his ball cap.

"I can see that. Part of a rogue agency that secretly monitors the main government. She looks like she's ready for anything. By the way, what's your friend's name, Turkeesha?" Sterling asks,

looking nerdier and needier than ever.

"Boys, this is my BFF, Cha-Cha, and she can compete with the best of 'em!" Turkeesha replies. We keep walking towards the park. As we get closer, we must pass a few creepy places. First, there's the cornfield with the spooky scarecrow. It's been here but keeps changing as someone cares for it. It's stuck on a pole like a giant cross, but the back sticks higher in the back for support, and a board across the main board to support the arms. Its eyes are black...well, cut-out holes that are. How it's dressed gives chills, especially the torn coat, which seems like it was just put on. And the head appears to follow you.

"Man, I don't like that thing. It makes me uncomfortable; I wouldn't say I like those boots. It seems wrong and doesn't belong here," Sterling says.

"It... It does seem like it wants to take you to a bad place. I wouldn't say I like the hat or the gloved hands. Look at how high the cornstalks are. You go in there; you'll need a flare gun to be found if you get lost," Turkeesha replies, still moving.

"I've never seen the farm owner, but those who have say he's weird. He doesn't talk to anybody, always looking like he's looking. I have a problem with the pants and shirt; you guys know what I mean!" Dexter says, looking nervous as well while clutching his bat close to his shoulder.

"Is it wearing skinny jeans? I think those are skinny jeans. Tell me those aren't skinny jeans on a scarecrow?" Cha-Cha asks.

"Well, let's just keep going. We've seen enough of this creeper. We still have to come back past him!" I say as we continue.

We pass the old steel mill. This is another place we've prepped for a fallback spot in case we need to fight some nasty nightcrawler. It's like a clubhouse, but the big three of us are still determining what it's being used for. Mr. Brown gave us specific equipment to stay ready, even the excellent hologram device to make it look rundown, and it can't be opened without one of us.

Final stop: we are here at Pettus Park. Let the games begin. This is our arena where we get down and dirty. This part of being a kid is just the best.

"So, what's the game today?" I ask. Dexter pulls a rubber ball and then a solid foam ball with some weight from his backpack.

"DODGE BALL, BABY! LET'S GO!" Dexter yells. Now, everybody line up against the wall to play coin toss to see who throws first." We all love Dodge Ball.

"You know the rules, mutants. If you are the thrower and the person you're trying to knock out catches the ball, you can be hit with it and put on the sideline. Got it?" Dexter asks; everyone is just anxious to get started.

The coin flips several times, and Sterling gets to throw it first. Now, we are lining up and preparing for Dodge Ball War.

"Okay, Dodge Ballers, what shall it be, foam or rubber?" Sterling asks, looking nervous as usual.

It doesn't take me long to decide because I understand the game and want to win. The choice of ball is easy; you go with the foam. It's easier to catch. The rubber can be as well if you have mongoose-like reflexes, which I do, but the foam is easier to see and send back. So, I say foam, and everybody agrees.

Sterling throws the first toss. It misses, bounces off the wall, and back to him. I know he wants to use his backpack from the academy. It has automation that would make him more of a ball- throwing beast, but that would give up our secret, which would be cheating.

We all know cheaters never win, but he gets loose. He wants to impress the girls, so he hits Cha-Cha in the foot. It bounces off her foot and catches Dexter's leg, to his delight. Now, you know that he has to brag.

"Check out my moves; two birds with one stone!" Sterling says. Boy, his youth slang is improving. It makes him sound less nerdy.

He goes at it again and hits Derron in the shoulder as he runs into Turkeesha. Derron slaps the wall, yelling, "MAN!" That lets us know he hated getting knocked out of the game. We go back and forth. I don't get knocked out, so I give my throws to the others. We play for a few more hours. Derron receives a call from his mother telling him that he needs to come home so they can go shopping for his dad's birthday gift. He knows what his dad wants, so he grabs his skateboard, waves at us, and takes the shortcut down "Handlebar Hill" to get there quicker. Man is moving down that hill, and then he's gone… out of sight.

The one thing I've never understood since I met the "Cootie Queen" is how on earth she's this good. Every time I'm not throwing, she's the last one standing. I know I get it. We all train at the academy, but you have something special for them to notice you. I can see that she has some excellent training. Dexter is flush red in the face because he can't hit her. This is the last game, and everybody is holding their breath. He wants to get even with her so badly that he's not focusing, which is the one thing they teach us all at the academy. She's like a cat on ice but in control.

Let me stop playing. If I were throwing at her and couldn't hit her, I'd be heated, too. But this is funny, watching him clench his fist. I haven't seen him this frustrated since the battle with "Pie Guy." But at last, it's over. She catches the ball and yells, "Game, big head!"

We look at each other and laugh, but then Dexter says, "Enough of this mess; let's go eat." We gathered the balls and headed to our favorite eating spot, Mr. Irving's. I can't wait as we joke and laugh there, but we all get quiet when we pass by the Scarecrow. It seems to follow you with its eyes as you pass by, and then it does the craziest thing.

"WHOA, did you see that? Did anybody see that?" I ask in shock. "See what, Crazy Crunch?" Dexter replies, gripping his bat.

"The head turned and looked at us, then quickly returned to where it started. I swear it moved!" I say, wanting to hit it or something.

"You are so weird. Let's keep going. I believe you're just hungry and seeing things now!" Turkeesha replies.

"Yeah, we're going to participate in the one event none of you 'Turkey Tongues' can beat me in EATING!" Dexter boasts. We keep moving, but I take out my slingshot, pick up a rock, and pop that spooky, straw-filled bum in the head, trying to knock its hat off.

"Come on, dude, let's get the good stuff. Nobody lights up the grill like Mr. Irving!" Sedale yells.

He's right. As I tried to shake off the eerie feeling that this Scarecrow kept giving me, I remembered my dad always teaching me many things that can be avoided if we trust our gut feelings. They help us avoid dangerous stuff, almost like a spider-sense. He even said it's been with us since man could first walk upright in Africa.

Well, my stomach is growling like a pit bull. I run to catch up with the others but take one last look back at the Scarecrow, thinking it will move. The only thing that moves is the raggedy clothing that covers it in the breeze. I know there's more to this thing than we're seeing. I know it.

Chapter 5

Virginia Woodard

Finally, we are here, and we've all brought our appetites. Opening the door triggers the alert bell, so we enter to find two tables but choose one large table, making us feel like "The Knights of the Round Table." We greet Mr. Irving, who is busy at the grill, with his back to us. He responds, "Hey, kids, how are you today? I'll be with you in a minute."

Me and Derron started going over the information we found on Satchel Crowson. The stuff we uncovered is pretty strange: he was a local cop in the '40s and was involved in some crooked activities, setting up people in ambush situations. He even made a pact with some evil cult that had been around here forever. He would lure people into dangerous places, then the cult would appear, and those people, some bad, some good, would never be heard from again. He even tricked some of his fellow cops into meeting the cult's demands. Eventually, he got sloppy, was caught, and sentenced to a hard time in prison.

While awaiting his sentence, the evil cult kidnapped him from his home and took him to Jackson Bridge. They had to ensure he wouldn't expose their existence. Despite his pleas, they weren't swayed. They stripped him of his clothes, tied his hands and feet, covered his head with a bag, attached a heavy rock to him, and pushed him off the bridge while cursing him. As he screamed and sank to the river's bottom, his fate was sealed. His body was found a week later.

"Wow, now that's a horrible way to go!" Cha-Cha says.

"No doubt, one of the worst. That cult didn't play," Dexter replies.

"Get this, guys. For years, you could hear him screaming on the foggiest nights, followed by a big splash until a spiritual cleansing was performed on the bridge. It used to terrify people," Sterling adds.

"Also, it says that a creepy scarecrow would mysteriously appear in town, and then people would go missing," Dexter notes.

"Alright, you guys ready to order? I will play a short-order cook and waiter today," Mr. Irving says as he takes out a pen and paper.

"Mr. Irving, sir, what do you know about a guy named Satchel Crowson and the creepy scarecrow over in the field down the way?" I ask.

"That name doesn't come up much. He was a disgrace, but his story is true as far as him being dealt with by that cult. But here's a twist: after they dumped him in the river, they created a straw man to capture his soul, binding him to it. People reported seeing this scarecrow chasing others, and those chased were never seen again. The town would destroy any scarecrows they found, eventually leading to a decrease in missing persons and a return to normalcy. Our town has a crazy history of bizarre events, but that scarecrow still gives me the willies. One day, it's there; the next, it's gone," Mr. Irving explains.

"Thank you, sir. I'm ready to order now. I'll have my usual, The Creature Crusher Combo, with apple cranberry juice!" I reply, and the gang is ready, too. But the story Mr. Irving just shared has left us a bit unsettled.

Dexter orders two of what I did, always going the extra mile but managing to devour it each time. Sterling opts for the Round Mound, a pasta and meatball dish. The girls chose The Suture Salad, one with grilled chicken and the other with fried chicken. Mr. Irving then returns to the kitchen and grill to start our orders.

"Well, I guess we can talk about what's going on. Sterling, how are those drone and remote bot improvements coming along?"

"I've downloaded plans for the drone camera by Marie Van Britton Brown, the woman who designed the first CCTV protocol. It shows how to scale down the camera size, making it lightweight. I've also been studying Jessie Russell, the inventor of the digital cell phone. What we'll gain from him is the ability to have unlimited range on both bots and drones, even through thick walls. He's currently working on 4G portable hotspots!" Sterling says.

"How long before you're finished, Booger Prince?" Dexter teases, eliciting laughter from the girls.

"Not long. All I gotta do is attach it to the drone and take it for a test run, which I will do when I get home; Locus Lips!" Sterling retorts, sending the girls into another fit of laughter.

He's so proud. Sterling has come a long way with his comebacks. He blushes and adjusts his glasses, the girls' admiration steaming up his lenses. But then, Cha-Cha says that she needs to go to the bathroom to wash her hands. This gives us a chance to finally talk about being unable to reach the academy. She wants Turkeesha to go with her, but Turkeesha pretends to drop something under the table and says she will catch up with her.

"Has anybody been able to get through to the academy yet?" I ask. "No," "Nope," and "Nah," they all reply.

"What do you think is blocking the signal?" Dexter asks.

"When I tried, all I got was thick static. It even turned my communicator off. It was so strong. But let me catch up with Cha-Cha before she gets back. It's a shame we can't tell everyone about what we do," Turkeesha replies.

"Whatever it is, it's strong enough to stop the most powerful information signals from getting in or out of our town. That, my friends, is impressive," Sterling says.

"I bet it's got everything to do with that scarecrow. I'll bet my academy badge on that!" I reply.

"Yep, it didn't start until all this popcorn rash mess started. I've been trying since we left the movies last night," Dexter says.

"I'm still thinking about Satchel Crowson. What did they turn him into? There's always a name those bad goofs get after trading in good for gangsta. Is he a 'Specter' or something?" I ask.

"Not according to the lore. A 'Specter' can only be created if a person is killed by a 'Wraith,' so no, he was done in by a devil cult that transformed him by combining his fear and hatred right at the time of his end. They've got the timing down since they've been doing this for a long time," Sterling replies.

"Well, how would we beat it down, you know? What are the weaknesses?" Dexter asks.

"Hmm, salt and silver, put them down for the count. Cutting off the head, they rarely touch the ground, but salt hurts them pretty badly," Sterling says, still looking at his LED screen.

"Seems like all supernatural baddies hate salt. It's one of the most potent Earth-based purifiers. Good thing we have an excellent supply of both, and we know how to use them," I add.

Turkeesha and Cha-Cha finally return to the table, and the food arrives. We have a blast for lunch, cracking jokes, keeping score, and just enjoying being kids who get outside and get dirty playing. We have kids talk about comic books, superheroes, sports, and what we want to be when we grow up—well, that part we know. On that part, we're just putting on a show for ChaCha.

We talk about being scientists, doctors, astronauts, cage fighters – guess who that one goes to. With our bellies full, we cleaned our table, took trash to the trash can, and thanked Mr. Irving for the great food. As we leave, he gives us the caring adult warning.

"Be careful out there. Watch out for each other. Many bad things are out there; I don't just mean people. That scarecrow is something different, so steer clear!" Mr. Irving says as he waves goodbye.

Well, now we have to decide which route to take home, and there are a few. I can't help wanting to go by and knock that dirty scarecrow off its perch and burn it up. A dirty old scarecrow, like we don't know what it is, is sitting there waiting for victims to jump on.

"I guess we'll see you 'Llama Lip boys' later. We're going home to write down the enormous amounts of victories we took today!" Turkeesha brags with their hands on her hips.

"You did all the work, so don't say 'we', 'Flamingo Face'!" she barely finished behind Sterling.

Dexter replies, rubbing his full belly, "You need to watch your mouth, tubby; looking like you got slapped with a bag full of cough drops!"

Cha-Cha says as we all burst out laughing. Even Mr. Irving had to laugh. We thought he was still in the store, but he just took out the trash.

"Let's go, girls. Smell, you boys, later. Oh, you may have won the most today, Sedale, but uh, it'll pass. I got you next time!" Turkeesha says.

"Beat it, Seal Face. You've got no chance against me. Go home and soak those big feet!" I reply. Why does she always have to say something to me? She sticks out her tongue as they get out of sight.

"So, you guys know what I'm thinking, right?" I ask, and they say yes. "Let's get that stupid scarecrow while there's daylight. Wraiths are helpless in direct sunlight, and it's only 3:17 PM."

"I don't have any salt, but I have some sage in my backpack, which I hear is pretty much the same!" Sterling replies.

"Yeah, let's spread some on them and around the base. Maybe by tomorrow, we can let the academy know what this thing is up to," Dexter says.

We get to the scarecrow and don't want to get too close, so I wrap the sage in my paper napkin pieces from lunch. We should've kept the salt packages. Dang it!

Well, we've got to work with what we've got now. I hit it and then around the base and say, "That should do it. Sage attack complete."

"Dude, that thing is smiling at us; check it out!" Dexter exclaims, and he's right. It is smiling and tapping its bony finger on the armrest supporting it.

"Guys, we should leave. We should be okay because there's still plenty of daylight out, and remember, wraiths are not a threat in broad daylight. But let's not wait to find out; what do you say, fellas?" Sterling says in a troubled tone.

We start to back away slowly. The daylight thing is right; its head is following us, but it looks like it's in pain doing that. As we move away, Dexter gives us an update.

"Hey, I almost forgot to tell you. We're going out of town for a day or two—the family, that is— so I won't be around to drag you two out of trouble. Make sure you lay low until the academy is back online," Dexter says.

"We're going to be fine. You make sure you do the same, pot belly!" Sterling replies. As we continue home, we all take one last hard look back and then at each other, wondering if that will hold it until we get the proper help from the academy. Still, I wish we had used salt, though.

Chapter 6

Birdie Daniels

Well, we make it home. Mom is there; she hugs me, and Dad is away on business. We talk about the dodgeball game and the creepy Scarecrow. She asks me if I let the academy know about it. I tell her that we all tried, but we keep getting static. She tells me to keep trying as she rubs her rash from the popcorn infection. I ask if she's okay; she says it's getting better. Mothers always try to downplay how bad a situation is. Mom adds another thing: Derron's mother called about 30 minutes ago to look for him. "I told her I'd ask you once you got home," she says. I told her the last time we saw him, he was heading home fast.

Mom said she sounded worried, as any mother would be. "Let me get started on dinner," she said.

I tell her okay, then go to my room. Sterling and I are about to play the latest online game, "Photon Black." It's a game where you can choose weapons, planets, and terrain. Your "Photon Black series 9" battle suit is experimental, state-of-the-art, and equipped to handle any environment. You can add flight, running speed, insane strength as you get better weapons, and just about anything you can ask for each stage as you face all sorts of creatures trying to spread infection before you meet the final boss.

Mom yells, "Dinner at 6; it's 4 PM, so we've got plenty of time to do what kids do…GAME HARD."

Sterling starts talking about the day. We've been gaming for about an hour when he begins to break down his rash, how it seems to be worsening, and what a Wraith indeed does.

"This rash is killing me. Itching awful for one minute, then nothing. I can't taste anything!" he says over the headset.

"Man, I'll be glad when the academy comes back online. Then we can tell them what's going on, and I'm sure they'll have a solution for the rash," I reply.

"Well, as far as Wraiths go, they must always make more. What they do is beat you up, then end you in some way, and then they compress and twist your soul and spirit, making you into one of them. But they need to put your soul into a vessel of their choice. These things seem to be very nasty. So, I was partially wrong about a Specter being the only way to create a Wraith. The problem is that there are many ways in the supernatural world to make one. Sheesh!" Sterling says.

"So they're vengeful and angry and have to make more. I got it. Man, we have to get the academy involved in this. I see that they can walk through walls and see through solid objects. These aren't the normal supernatural baddies!" I replied, wondering what to do if we can't get the academy online.

"Nope, they are top tier on the list, well at least top 10, but that's still pretty bad. My parents won't let me out until the academy can be reached and we clear this thing up, so no school for me tomorrow!" Sterling says sadly.

"Dawg, don't be such a nerd. Enjoy that time off," I reply.

We make it to a good point in the game when Mom calls out, "Dinner time, let's go, young man." I tell Sterling that I have to go. We saved the game and signed off, and I told him about Derron before we got off the headset. I tell him I'll let him see what goes down, so stand by; then we end the conversation.

Mom and I have a great dinner talk. I ask her about Derron; she says his mother called and said he's back but acting strange, but he's home, she says.

I ask when Dad will be back and when we will let him in on the academy.

"He should be back tonight when you're asleep, and I guess we'll tell him in due time. Mr. Brown says he'll tell him better when the men discuss this. It's funny, though, how I think he knows something. Your father is not a dumb man; he's very sharp," she replies as she puts the dishes in the sink.

She started to rub her rash, so I tried to help her, but she said no. "I don't know if this thing is catching, so go get your shower and get ready for school tomorrow. I've got this, but thanks, sweetie," she says. As I hit the shower, it's relaxing, and the soap smells good. We had a great day, I think to myself. As I dry off, I put a little lotion on my body so I'm not ashy, brush my teeth, and finish. I yell to Mom, "Goodnight," and go to my room, jump on the bed face first. I roll over on my back and begin to doze off.

I'm awakened by Rosco barking loudly, trying to break his chain. Then I hear a loud noise downstairs, like there's a fight going on. I jump up, grab my slingshot, and run downstairs; then I get the scare of my life. I see my mother floating above the kitchen floor, close to the spice rack, kicking. I see them closer: two eerie, large ghost hands have her around her upper arms. The hands are coming out of the wall, picking her up. Out of nowhere, a face I'd seen earlier peers through above my mother's head, finally coming all the way through, still holding her up. IT'S THE SCARECROW!

I'm shocked but also angry at the same time. I aim with my slingshot and yell, "Let her go NOW CREEP!"

"Now, isn't this a surprise? She has the rash mark, and I've come to collect her. The look on your face is priceless. It would help if you had left well enough alone, boy. If you don't mind, I'll take what's mine!" the phantom says. You can feel the evil emanating from this thing.

As he tries to pull my mother through the wall, she blacks out. I have to think fast. "No, Butter Lips, you won't be taking my mom. Not now, not ever." Just then, I aim. I see the salt container on the spice rack. I let a rock fly, hitting my mark. The container bursts open, and the salt flies over the phantom's face and arms. It screams so loud it shakes the whole house, but it drops Mom and ghosts back through the wall. I run to her to make sure she's okay. I drag her to the living room. I'm so glad for physical fitness training; this would be tough if I weren't in shape. Great, she's still breathing, just unconscious, but the rash is glowing. I know it's still here, so I hit the emergency button that links me to Sterling and Dexter. I get ready with my slingshot. I've dipped a few of my sticky rocks in the salt. This thing does hate salt, but I can see it darting through one wall after another. I've got to stay steady.

I wish I had grabbed more salt from the kitchen, but most were busted up, and now I don't have time to get it. I have some stuff that we have been working on for things like this. I'm not going

to be able to make it upstairs, though. Here it comes; it's just walking through the wall and the furniture.

"I will take what's mine. She ate the ritual foods, and now she has the mark. Do not stand between me and what's mine, or I will make you suffer!" the Scarecrow says in a raspy voice, floating about the room.

"You won't be taking anything in this house, not tonight or ever. This is my mother, my home, and nothing is going to stop or touch them without getting the $10.99 butt whoop special. I've got yours ready to go, bro, and yours is ready for takeout!" I reply, I've never been so determined or focused to stop something. This is my mother, and I'm the man of the house when Dad's not around. I'm not scared one bit, either.

"Child, your mouth is chaotic at best. Now, feel the wrath of my rage!" he yells, and the force pushes me back. Mom slowly slides back but stops against the sofa.

This is the anger wraiths have; they are filled with it. The yell forces the furniture, myself included, to fly against the wall hard. I get the wind knocked out of me. I'm stunned and can't move. He's messed up my equilibrium. I need to find out which way is up. I can only hear his laughter getting closer. I try to aim with my slingshot, but I can't focus. I can't use my wrist shots either; they won't activate without connection with the academy like a child lock safety measure. Here he comes. He laughs, pulls out a vast burlap-type bag, and says in the most trashy voice I can describe, "I'll be taking what's mine. Be lucky it was just a dream for you." He grabs my mother by the arm and stuffs her in the bag.

"Don't touch her!" I yell, still trying to shake off the rage cry he hit me with.

"Or what? Don't you think that request is a bit late, considering I already have it in the bag? I'll be seeing you later. Your mom is going to make great fertilizer!" The Scarecrow replies as it fades through the door with my mother on its back. It looked back at me again, smiling, and tipped its hat to me, then wholly walked through the door as if it wasn't there.

Then Sterling comes through using our communication link. "Sedale, Sedale, come on, man, I just got your alert. Man, answer me!" Sterling says as I try to get on my feet and stop the room from spinning.

"I'm here, and he took my mom. The Scarecrow took my mom. She had the rash. As the legend says, they keep their numbers going by spreading that rash and making more wraiths. I'm going to get her back. I'll send Roscoe over with that canister we've been working on. I will bust open the Tri-wagon to go after him, so stand by!" I reply as I get everything ready as fast as I can.

"Oh, man, not your mom. That's not cool. He's going to pay for this. Wait, I've got it too, the rash!" Sterling says in an angry voice.

"You got that double right. We may not have all the good stuff of the LLA, but we make stuff good with what we have. Attach the canister to the drone and follow me when you get hooked. I placed a tracker in Mom's shoe, and it's active, so I'm…out. Roscoe's on his way, and I'm hunting for Scarecrows!" I yell as I explode from our garage on my modified wide-bed ATV.

Chapter 7

Kenneth Shipp

I've got my earphones on, bumping "Ante Up" by MOP. It gets me excited. I'm going as fast as I can; the signal is strong. By the arms of Ogun, that scarecrow is going to pay for taking my mom. My dad said I'm the man of the house when he's gone. I feel like I've let him down. I know he means within limits, but still, his most precious thing in the world is in great danger, and she was taken on my watch. I zip in and out on the back roads, taking me to the old cornfield from earlier. The ATV I'm driving is modified to expand into a flatbed; that's how we got all the materials to our secret safe houses all over town. It even has remote homing driving capabilities, just in case. Let me check with Sterling to see if he's ready.

"Hey, Sterling, did you get it yet?" I ask. He answers right away.

"Yeah, got it hooked up. You should see the drone any minute now; it's zoomed in on your location. I can monitor your situation from the camera mounts. Plus, Roscoe's going back home. Seems like you're heading back to the cornfield. Oh man, that place was scary, even in the daytime. We've got our work cut out for us this time!" Sterling replies as the drone with the canister attached flies in.

I let him know that the drone is here and that I can see it. I ask him to test the canister and spray me. He does. Then he tells me that there are two spots where my mom might be: an old barn on the right and straight ahead, where my tracker is giving off her location. But I need to catch this bum off guard so he can't get the drop on me. After all, I'm on his turf. I decide to take the barn approach, then circle to my mom's location, as Mr. Brown says, "Flank 'em."

The corn is high, man, and a sweet smell is coming out of the air. I push through as quietly as I can. Sterling has to be my eyes because I'm moving in blind on this one. He has the high ground.

I can see the drone moving smoothly and quietly, making no noise, just like my ATV. It's in stealth mode, running on battery power, and makes no sound. It's not bad for two eleven-year-old geniuses. I get to the barn, jump off the ATV, run inside, and see tools, food in jars, and the name in my dream: Satchel Crowson, next to a hat and long coat. Who labels stuff this way?

I let Sterling know there's no sign of my mother, so I'm moving over to the ping the tracker gives off. The drone dials in on it and moves in that direction. I hop back onto the ATV, and Sterling tells me I can't miss the spot. It's about one hundred yards straight ahead, and there are three scarecrows on posts with open pits in front of them. Wait, one has a little dirt in it! Sterling says.

I go through a vast spot where all the corn is laid flat in a pattern, and I mean huge, but I don't have time to check it out, so I keep going. I can see the drone hovering and blinking where my tracker says my mom is. I see three tall corn stalks, the ones Sterling was talking about. Two of the stalks are big... You can say giant ears of corn?

"What are they?" Sterling asks as the drone hovers around them, trying to get readings.

"I don't know, but my tracker says this is the spot. There are two empty slots and one covered with dirt, but not all the way. The two empty slots have clothes in the bottom, laid out as if people were there, and where there should be a head, feet, and arms, there's only some gray dust. There's also a tube at the point of the stalks. Man, I have to find Mom. The signal is powerful here at the last cornstalk. I'm going to start digging. Watch my back," I reply.

I get to work digging as fast as I can. When I come to a bump in the dirt, I get cautious and start moving the dirt away slower. There's a face with a mask and a breathing tube. IT'S MY MOTHER! I take the mask off and drag my mom out of the hole. She's breathing, just dirty.

"Sterling, I've found her. I'm going to put her on the ATV. Give me a second!" I say.

"You might want to hurry up. The signal coming towards you is ice cold, which means something supernatural is coming, which means the Wraith and those other two cornstalks lit up, too. A cold signature, just like the Wraith, coming your way, moving fast!" Sterling replies, as I've got my mom ready to take back home. I keep thinking I'm going to make this bum pay. I hit the auto drive to take my mom back home; it will take her through the garage to safety.

"Ok, mom's on her way home. I can see the cornstalk husks start to peel away. I blow on a whistle that makes no sound. I need a backup because the Wraith is now here, and he looks mad, holding a sickle like he's the Grim Reaper or somebody. 'A little late cutting the grass, don't you think, corn cob?' It floats above, coldly staring at me, and

39

it's evident that the stalks are his minions of doom as they fall to the ground, trying to stand on wobbly legs.

'You're hard to track, and it's strange you know some people. Plus, you're courageous enough to challenge me with my new Wraiths behind you. I may have lost your mother, but you'll do. I can always retrieve her!' it says, floating towards me.

'And you're courageous in showing an ugly face. I'm expecting back up any minute now, and I know some people!' I say, just as we can hear something tearing through the cornfield. It's Roscoe, and he looks ready. But watch this!

'A dog, a big simple dog. You've got to be joking. We are going to tear you up!' The Wraith replies.

'This isn't just any dog. This one is trained to fight mop heads like you, cats!' I pat Roscoe and then hit the button on his dog collar. Now, this is the only tech that works without the LLA. It, piece by piece, starts to cover Roscoe in a silver and Teflon coating, which will allow him to tear into ghost butts. The term 'BEAST' clearly fits him. It even covers his jaws and paws.

'SILVER... YOU HAVE SILVER!?' The Wraith says, sounding nervous. 'You've made this personal, and I have two words for you. SIC' EM!'

Roscoe turns and tears into the two new Wraiths. I start slingshot bananas on the leader; the salt burns them, while Roscoe's silver-armored body allows him complete success. All I can hear are growls and screams from the monsters. I also added silver nitrate powder to my Shock Rocks slingshot and weapons. The Wraith blocks some of my shots while swinging its sickle, taking down a lot of corn in one swipe. But I dodge and roll out of the way, giving the bum a shot between the eyes. You can see smoke coming out of its face as it rips off its hat, throws it on the ground, and then starts rubbing its face hard, trying to get my Shock Rocks out of its eyes.

"How does fear taste, bio waste?" I yell. But then Sterling reminds me that we must get him to the bridge, to one of the safe spots we've set up all over town.

"Bro, get out of there. I don't think you can stop him on his turf. Follow the drone; I'll lead you out. That sickle is no joke; one hit and you will be doomed. Let's move while he's distracted. The bridge isn't that far from where you are!" he says.

"Right," I call out to Roscoe. I can see that he's beaten up one of the new Wraiths and has the other one down, violently shaking it. But when I call him, he lets go and runs to me. I look at the last Wraith, and it's allergic to the silver fangs on Roscoe's armor; it has turned into a bubbling pile of white pus. Yuck! We tear through the cornstalks, looking up and following Sterling's drone, and he leads us to a clearing where we can see the road. But behind us, it's cutting everything. All I can see is corn flying in the air. We quickly turn; now, I can see the bridge. This has to be a shortcut from a different direction. It doesn't matter, though; now we do it my way.

Each swing and miss from the Wraith's sickle tears up the road, and chunks fly everywhere. We are almost to the bridge when Sterling comes through my comlink.

"Sedale, I've made contact with Mr. Brown. He's sending a team to back us up. I told him about the communication blackout. ETA about 30 minutes; that's all you gotta hold out for!" Sterling says.

But just as I think we will make it, I'm frozen and lifted into the air. I can't move as I'm thrown back into the cornfield. Roscoe jumps and breaks my fall. I know now that this is terrible, very bad. We can't see the Wraith now because the cornstalks are thick. We keep looking around. I look up and see the drone; it's wobbly and then falls to the dirt. That's not good because I need it to guide us out. I grab it, pick it up, and realize the cover has been knocked loose; the RAM card cracked on impact. Luckily, I have a spare. This was 8 bits on a 64-bit operating system. I have a RAM card with 16 gigabytes with me. I insert it into the card slot, and the drone lights up, ready for round two. I told Sterling that the upgrade was the best option. There is nothing like testing a theory in the field of battle.

"Yo, Sterling," I whisper. "He's pulled me back into the corn. The drone was damaged. I replaced it with the 16-gigabyte RAM card. Look at how it's moving and responding now. I told you; see, look at that performance!"

"Wow, it is, and the response is incredible. If you survive this, maybe I'll pay for the next meal!" Sterling says.

Just then, Roscoe starts growling and takes a defensive stance. That could only mean one thing:

Crowson is here. The drone scans for its energy signature and immediately locates it. He's looking for us, but he's released more popcorn boys to get us. Oh man, it's time to end this.

"Sterling, is that emitter working, or was it damaged in the fall?" I ask.

"No, according to the diagnostics, it's working fine. What do you have in mind, bro?" Sterling responds.

"I've noticed that these clones he's making have a lot of popcorn. A lot of popcorn. I will activate the microwave beam, pop them, then do the same to the field to buy me some cover to get out. I will send Roscoe home to protect Mom," I reply.

"Okay, gotcha. Let's do it. He's coming to you; get ready. I'll start targeting the clones right about… NOW!" Sterling says as he starts firing the microbursts at the clones, which works. They become Jiffy Pop boys, and Roscoe pounces on them individually, finishing them off in a flash of brilliance.

"Roscoe, boy, I need you to go home. Protect mom; she needs you. Now go, boy, go home!" He tried to lick my face and whined a bit, then I gently pushed him toward home, and he darted off.

Now, to finish the task at hand. My tracker alerts me that the Wraith is coming, so I give Sterling the okay to FIRE, and he does, hitting the cornstalks. The whole area turns into a popcorn paradise. Wow, the popcorn is so high; I never thought it could get that high. This is good; now it can't see me. The Wraith screams. I escape, running out of the field and to the bridge as fast as possible.

I make it to the bridge and shout to the Wraith, "Let's go Joe," and the drone catches up to me. "Or are you just going to stay playing in the field, waiting for butter for your popped corn clones?" He's seen Derrons and me angry, and now he's coming to finish what he started.

I run to the middle of the bridge, and he swings his sickle. I tuck and roll just in time as he destroys a bridge section, exposing the river below. He managed to get on the side of the bridge that I was on.

"I've got you now, chump. You know you can't cross over running water, so come get me, moron!" I yell.

"Oh, I'll do more than that. You're going to be my greatest trophy. That fighting spirit will serve me for centuries!" The Wraith says, and he comes streaking forward. I turn to run to get to the other side, where we can trap him.

Suddenly, I hear, "DUCK, GOOSE!" It's Dexter. He swings his bat against the side of the wall, dropping the silver-laced net on the phantom. It struggles, and I trigger the mini-explosions that will collapse the bridge, dropping the phantom into the water and trapping it there forever.

However, the bridge only partially falls apart. The phantom begins to crawl towards me, and then Dexter, with a mighty slam of his bat, causes the bridge to continue breaking down.

"CHECKMATE, GREMLIN GUT! THIS IS FOR MOM!" I shout. I jump up as high as I can and stomp down, finally bringing the bridge tumbling down. The phantom falls into the water, screaming on the way down. The water is charged with blue, red, and yellow lights; then, everything goes calm as the light show drifts downriver before it finally fades out.

"I thought you were heading out of town!" I ask Dexter, fist-bumping him.

"Yeah, we did, but the family disagreed. I was trying to reach you guys, but when I heard what was happening, I raced here as quickly as possible. That one was a nasty piece of work!" Dexter replies, leaning on his bat. Right on time, Mr. Brown and the cleanup crew arrive in full force.

Some hang from helicopters, dropping stuff into the water, then picking up a solid block form that glows.

"You young men, alright? You seem to have everything under control," Mr. Brown asks in his calm tone, as usual.

"Yes, sir, thank you!" We both respond.

"The phantom was powerful enough to blackout communications for a city, which is pretty impressive. We got here as soon as we could. Sterling, can you brief me? We need to get Sedale home to his mother; he's had a formidable day," Mr. Brown requests. What's weird is that he talks directly to Sterling without any visible devices. What kind of tech is he using?

"Yes, sir, sending the upload now!" Sterling replies.

"The drone is a nice touch. You all have shown great teamwork. We'll take it from here. We won't leave you young men alone like this again. You will never be alone if you stay true to each other. And as you can see, evil never works alone. Let's get you home. They'll repair the bridge, and the cornfield will be examined and destroyed. Hopefully, we can do something for the surviving victims," Mr. Brown says.

"Sir, what is that light over the cornfield?" I ask, but it's gone as soon as Mr. Brown and Dexter look.

"Sterling, can you fly the drone over the cornfield so we can see if there's any trace of that light?" I ask. He does, and what we see is a crop circle. Mr. Brown says, "Hmm," enough for one day. "Let's get you young men home," he continues, studying the image on my screen. I've been around him long enough to notice when he says, "Hmm," it's a severe sign of something to come. But we leave, for that is the end of Satchel Crowson. The cleanup crew will sanitize any residual effects.

Chapter 8

Michale Hobson

We finally made it back home. Mr. Brown checks on my mom and talks with my dad for a few minutes, giving him the usual cover story about what happened. I used that break to speak to my mother.

"I'm so proud of you. You did exactly as your father told you to be my best protection, plus you defended me like no mother could ever ask from a son. You truly were the man of the house.

This will be our little secret; you know how it goes!" Mom says as she grabs me, hugging the life out of me. Mr. Brown leaves, nods at me, then tips his hat. Then, Dad rubs my head and sits beside Mom, holding her in his arms.

I climb out of my window to sit on the roof, staring at the stars, thinking about how I almost lost Mom today. That scares me. Who knew there were all these monsters out in the world? Maybe one or two, but Mr. Brown says I have no idea what's out in the dark places of the universe.

That's why they recruit us to have an army to fight for humanity forever, as long as there are monsters. Then, my Comlink goes off. I think, "Man, another mission so soon?" But that's not it. It's Poofy Puffs.

"Ok, what is it now, Poofy Puffs?" I ask.

"That was a brave thing you did tonight. Sterling filled me in. No fooling around. I know I give you a hard time, but I'm being real right now. Fighting that thing to get your mom back took guts.

I hope that if I'm called on to do the same, I won't fold, which I doubt I would. However, family involvement in our work could change things, especially when emotions run high. You came through like a champ, even though you have a great big PUMPKIN HEAD!" Turkeesha says.

"Thanks, I guess. You always have to throw a joke in, don't you? I hope I never have to go that route again. I was scared to tell you the truth. It was cut off from our best tech, and there was no way to contact the Academy. It was rough. Sterling and Roscoe are the best wingmen. I can't leave out Dexter; in the end, he was solid!" I reply.

"Well, it wouldn't be me if I didn't say something silly, now would it? I do have a different level of respect for you. You are the best of us. I'll knock you back to the Kushite Dynasty if you tell anybody I said that. Catch you later, smelly gator!" Turkeesha says before signing off.

Something else that caught my attention: why does it always seem like my dad and Mr. Brown know each other when they talk? It's bizarre. And now, Sterling is buzzing my radio.

"What you got?" I ask.

"Well, this is what the drone picked up on the light in the cornfield. These are crop circles, and I've looked on the internet, cross-checked them, and they don't seem to match any images,"

Sterling says.

"These are some strange images. Does Mr. Brown have these images?" I reply.

"Yeah, he got the feed linked to the Academy. I wonder what he thinks about these shots. Just look at how quickly the light was there, then gone," Sterling says.

"So, what do you dweebs think these are? And we know that they are aliens?" Dexter chimes in.

"We can't assume they are aliens; they could be extra-dimensional. We'll have to wait and see... Well, thanks for the update. This has been a long day; I want to sleep," I reply.

"Ok, I'm out. See you guys tomorrow," Dexter says. "Me too. Catch you cats later," Sterling replies.

I have to make sense of this for now. I take one more look at the clear night sky. A few shooting stars streak across the sky. I thank the heavens for pulling us through this day. Man, this is what we do: getting ready to battle and being the frontline against all the evil out there. It's wild, but I wouldn't trade this for anything. And to think that we thought Dexter was the worst bully out there... He has nothing on these things that keep popping up one after the other.

My dad always says, "There is always someone bigger and worse." In this case, he was meaner and scarier than we thought. Oh boy, how right he was!

This book is dedicated to

Yolonda Trice.

Sabrina Griffin.

Uncle Carl.

Jahreal Victor James.

Laquita Killebrew.

Lewis Hopper.

Carl Chambliss.

Tim Thompkins.

Kenneth Shipp.

Alice Davis.